The Moral Statistics Of France

A new impulse has recently been given to statistical research. At the meeting of the British Association at Cambridge in 1833, a *statistical section* was engrafted upon the Association, principally through the zealous exertions of a distinguished foreigner, M. Quételet of Brussels. Subsequently and through the efforts of this section, a General Statistical Society has been formed in London, which has the Marquis of Lansdown for its President, and enrols among its members many of our public men, the most distinguished for enlightened patriotism and scientific attainments. It is the aim of this Society to encourage the formation of branches in every part of the kingdom. In Manchester a Statistical Society was still earlier formed, and the communications which have been made by its members, particularly by Mr. W. R. Greg, to the British Association, are evidence of the zeal and talent with which its proceedings are conducted.*

The object of the *Statistical Society* is simple, but comprehensive. Its motto might be the admirable and well-known aphorism of Lord Bacon, which M. Guerry prefixes to his work: "Homo, naturæ minister et interpres, de naturæ ordine tantum scit et potest quantum *observaverit*, nec ampliùs scit aut potest."—(Nov. Org.)

Statistical science does not intrude on the province of moral and political philosophy. It deals not with the powers and affections of our nature, as to their essential character and relations, but only investigates the numerical laws developed in their external effects and operations; thus giving, as Professor Sedgwick says, "the *raw material* to political economy and political philosophy," and helping to lay a firm *foundation* for those sciences. The Society announces that its aim is "to procure, arrange, and publish facts, calculated to *illustrate the condition and prospects of society*." Its first and most essential rule is to exclude what is merely *opinion*, to confine its attention rigorously to facts, and as far as possible to such facts as can be stated numerically, and arranged in tables. In the collection and arrangement of these facts, and in reducing the laws which they display to "the order, the harmony, and the consistency of theory," great patience and labour are required; the field of investigation is almost boundless; and it is only from very numerous and diversified observations that general results can safely be deduced.

Rich as is the history of the human mind in the department of rash speculation, it would be difficult perhaps to find instances of greater absurdity, and more marked contempt of experience and scientific research, than the records of *legislation* display. The most intricate and momentous questions, affecting the well-being of millions, have been settled at all hazards, according to the prejudices of the day, with little or no regard to

* It is gratifying to find that an office has recently been opened at the Board of Trade, for the collection and publication of official documents connected with statistical subjects.

the evidence of facts, or to those fundamental laws of human action, which must eventually control and modify all conventional rules.* We must ascribe this in certain cases to the necessity of fixing *some* laws—be they good or bad—before the condition of a people can become the subject of statistical investigation; but the grand source of this anomaly, in all ages and countries, has been the struggle of private interests, or the conflict of political passions, when the welfare of the whole community should be recognised as the only proper rule and standard. "In moral and political reasoning," it has been well said, "we have ever to do with questions in which the waywardness of man's will, and the turbulence of man's passions, are among the strongest elements." It is of the greatest consequence then when such weighty interests are at stake, to give moral and political philosophy the sound basis of *facts*, and to assimilate their processes, as far as possible, to those of demonstrative science. We all recollect the famous saying of Hobbes, "that if it had been a thing *contrary to the* [supposed] *interests of men* that the three angles of a triangle should be equal to two right angles, that doctrine would have been, if not disputed, yet suppressed, as far as they whom it concerned were able."

But all arguments against *experience* are fallacious; and in physical truth (to quote again Professor Sedgwick's words), "Whatever may be our difference of opinion, there is an ultimate appeal to experiment and observation, against which passion and prejudice have not a single plea to urge." Why then should not our moral and political reasoning, so far as practicable, be made subject to the same criterion? Complex and diversified as are the motives that influence the human will and

"Human action,
That is the seed too of contingencies
Strew'd on the dark land of futurity,"

their general results in the character and condition of society may legitimately be classed within the province of inductive science. These results are susceptible in a great degree of being reduced to measurement and

* "No advantage in moral policy can be lasting, which is not founded on the indelible sentiments of the heart of man. Whatever law deviates from that principle will always meet with a resistance, which will destroy it in the end."—Beccaria on Crimes and Punishments (quoted by Simpson, "On Popular Education," p. 280).

The same principle is strongly urged by Dr. Hampden in his "Lectures on Moral Philosophy;" an almost invaluable book to the student of human nature, and full of the elements of thought. "Ignorance of the nature of man, and of his condition in this world, will be found at the bottom of those wild theories of the regeneration of society and revolutions of government, which speculatists or the seditious have devised." . . . "How much vain disturbance, how much severe suffering, might have been saved, had a diffused knowledge of the principles of human nature established a general conviction, that there were impossibilities in the moral no less than in the physical world!"—pp. 55, 61.

calculation; and unquestionably will be found to develope general laws, no less remarkable and worthy of investigation than those which obtain in the physical universe.

It is incredible how much the world has lost, from the neglect of those inquiries which it is the object of the Statistical Society to promote. How much pernicious legislation might have been checked,—how many ruinous and sanguinary wars avoided,—how much crime prevented, and happiness diffused, had it been the constant care of each community to collect and give publicity to those facts, which demonstrate the real causes of a nation's prosperity, and exhibit the practical results of its institutions! The extent, productions, and resources, of a country,—the population, mortality, and rate of increase, the occupation of the different classes, and the distribution of wealth among them,—the state of the currency and taxation, the progress of agriculture, commerce, and manufactures,—the condition of the poor,—the state of education, religious instruction, and of crime,—are all matters that come within the province of statistical inquiry; and could a people be well disciplined in a knowledge of their actual condition in these various respects, it could not fail, under the blessing of Providence, to introduce more harmony into their social conduct, to establish the true civil policy of the country, and in every way to advance its prosperity.*

We might give many and striking instances of the disgraceful neglect of statistical research in England, and of the errors and inconsistencies, both of legislation and practical statesmanship, which have resulted from this neglect. We can here, however, only refer to the remarks of other writers on the same subject, which will be found too amply justified by facts.†

Statistics have been conveniently divided into *four* general classes,—*economical*, *political*, *medical*, and *moral*. The three former of these divisions embrace the facts relating to the productions and wealth of a country, its political and civil institutions, the laws of population, mortality, &c.; and to these elements statistical inquiries (scanty as they are at best) have been hitherto restricted. The subject of *moral* Statistics is emphatically

* "When we look beyond the range of physical tangibilities, into the region of mental and moral relations, in short the science of man, upon which depend the wisdom of our legislation, and the soundness of our institutions and customs, what a scene of uncertainty do we see! Fixed principles in social affairs have not yet been attained. . . . . If any measure affecting the public is propounded, there arises a perfect hurricane of opposition and denunciation, as if it were the most monstrous of errors, and the most atrocious of crimes. No plan or project, religious, civil, economic, or merely ornamental, can be proposed without tearing to pieces the conventions of courtesy—nay, the feelings of common charity, and exposing a lamentable scene of inconsistency and passion."—Simpson on Pop. Educ. p. 40.

† Edinb. Rev. xlix. 413, lxi. 158. For. Quart. Rev. xvi. 211, &c.

man,* in some of his most interesting social relations, and especially as an agent responsible to his fellows. The first step in the formation of political society is the institution of certain laws, and the transference of power and authority to some one or more of the community, to enforce their observance under suitable penalties. The great end of all civil institutions is the due protection of person and property, in other words the establishment of the *rights* of all. Mr. Hume informs us,† that "we are to look upon all the vast apparatus of our government as having ultimately no other object or purpose but the distribution of *justice*, or in other words, the support of the twelve judges: kings and parliaments, fleets and armies, officers of the court and revenue, ambassadors, ministers and privy councillors, are all subordinate in the end to this part of the administration."

Without an intimate acquaintance, however, with the facts coming under the head of the Statistics of Crime, penal legislation must be a course of blind and hazardous experiment. We shall not know either the amount of moral evil with which society has to contend, or where existing checks and preventives require to be strengthened. No government, therefore, can stand excused, which neglects the establishment of the data that are required to give a proper direction to criminal jurisprudence, and to advance safely in the work of national improvement.

M. Guerry's work relates wholly to the department of *moral* Statistics; and we are indebted to him as being the first to exhibit, in a systematic form, the principal facts illustrating the social condition of one of the great European Powers. France offers particular advantages for investigations of this nature. Since the year 1792, when the custody of the registers was transferred from the ecclesiastical to the civil authorities, they have been kept with great care and exactness in respect to those facts which develope the laws of population and mortality: but the earliest published documents relating to the administration of criminal justice that can be relied on, do not date earlier than 1825. It is now the custom in France for the Procureurs Généraux (officers nearly corresponding to the Procurators Fiscal of the Scotch courts) to transmit, every three months, to the Keeper of the Seals an accurate register of the business of the local judicial courts. These returns are classified on a systematic plan, and, after careful examination, an analysis is made of them at the end of each year, and published under the title of "Compte général de l'administration de la justice criminelle." The very rigid system of police established in France, and the superior intelligence of the functionaries to whose custody criminals are committed, combined with the centralising controul exercised

* "That comprehensive atom!—all the world
In act of thought embracing; in the world
A grain, scarce filling a particular space!"
Phil. Van Artev. ii. 221.

† Essays, i. 32.

by the higher branches of government, (however objectionable on some grounds) have undoubtedly the effect of enabling that government to collect the Statistics of Crime, in a far more complete and scientific form than is practicable under the existing arrangements in this country. And it is, I believe, with truth that M. Guerry remarks, "Never among any people has an undertaking of the kind been executed in a manner so complete:" and, though as yet little known in France itself, this digest of facts has rightly obtained from foreigners the appellation of a national monument, and has been viewed as a model for the imitation of all civilised nations, who have any desire to be acquainted with their moral condition. Many of the European states indeed are now following the example of France, but few of them have as yet adopted a system so comprehensive and exact.

Favoured perhaps by his situation as an advocate in the royal court, M. Guerry has availed himself of all the official documents bearing upon his subject, and has combined and classified them under all the various aspects they can be made to assume. His essay was published in 1833, having been first submitted to the French Institute, by whom as usual it was referred to a committee consisting of M. M. Lacroix, Silvestre, and Girard. The reporter of the committee (M. Girard) bears strong testimony to the fidelity with which our author has treated his subject, and especially to his entire freedom from bias to particular systems—a matter of no slight moment in a compiler of statistical tables. His conduct on this point indeed is worthy of all praise and imitation.*

The official returns, which form the ground-work of M. G.'s volume, relate to *crimes*, as modified by sex, age, and season, their apparent causes, their relative frequency, and geographical distribution; the state of *instruction* throughout France, of charitable *benefactions*, and the number and distribution of *suicides*, besides a mass of other particulars which M. G. ha condensed in an appendix.

We must notice that the estimates of the number and proportions of crimes are not founded on the number of the *convicted*, but on that of the *accused*, it being of no consequence as to the statistical result, whether the accused in each case is the guilty party or not, so long as the crime itself is established as a fact. From the formalities necessary before a case can come before a jury in France, (which are even greater than among ourselves) M. G. estimates that out of 1000 cases brought before the courts of Assize, there are scarcely 20 in which the acquittal of the

* "Aucun esprit de système ne nous a dirigé, nous n'avons cherché d'appui à aucune théorie. C'eût été montrer des vues peu philosophiques, et mal comprendre les intérêts de son pays, que de s'attacher à faire ressortir les faits favorables à une doctrine en négligeant ceux que lui paraissaient contraires. Nous avons d'ailleurs fait connaître avec soin les sources où nous avons puisé, et donné ainsi les moyens de s'assurer de notre exactitude et de notre sincérité."—Pref. p. iii.

accused has arisen from defective proof of the actual commission of the crime. On the other hand, were the state of crime estimated only from the number of persons *convicted*, the errors would probably be serious.*

It would be a task of great interest to compare together the criminal Statistics of different states, but as yet there are insuperable difficulties in the way. As a preliminary requisite, we must establish a common standard of legislative morality, and an uniform activity in the executive police. From differences in these respects, the statistical records of one country may shew a much smaller amount of crime than those of another, where perhaps no real superiority exists: and without bearing these considerations in mind, we should fall into great errors in comparing different epochs in the history of a nation, or the morality of different countries at the same period.

It appears that on the average, 72 out of 100 accused are connected either by birth or residence with the department in which they are brought to trial. This proportion increases to 84 in 100, in respect to crimes against the *person*, and falls to 69 in 100 as to offences against *property*. Not above 3 in 100, of the accused throughout France, are found to be foreigners.

To give value and certainty to Criminal Statistics, it is necessary to arrange and combine facts, so as to divest them of whatever is merely accidental. Adopting this principle, M. G. assures us that general results can be established, so uniform and constant as to preclude the supposition of their mere fortuitous recurrence.† In proof of this position, M. G. in the first place institutes a comparison between the number of crimes committed within a given period, in different parts of the kingdom. For sta-

* The criminal records of our own country confirm the opinion, that the number of *convictions* only affords very inadequate data from which to estimate the amount of crime. It is constantly found that the proportion of *convictions* to *committals* is greatest in the case of offences, of which the punishment is least severe. Thus in 1832, out of 107 persons committed for arson, only 35 were convicted; and for murder, out of 66 committed, only 20 were convicted; while for larceny, 10,130 convictions were obtained out of 13,469 committals. In Scotland the whole number of acquittals and liberations bears a considerably higher ratio to the committals than in England; and this arises from the very large number who in Scotland are liberated without ever being brought to trial, being very nearly 1-3 of the whole committals, instead of about 1-7, as in England. It is understood, however, that by far the greater number of these persons are so liberated, not because they are believed to be innocent, or even because there would be any difficulty in proving their guilt, but under the feeling that they are sufficiently punished by their incarceration previous to the time of trial. (Vide British Almanack and Companion for 1834, p. 66.)

† "Chaque année voit se reproduire le même nombre de crimes dans le même ordre, dans les mêmes regions; chaque classe de crimes a sa distribution particulière et invariable, par sexe, par âge, par saison: tous sont accompagnés, dans des proportions pareilles, de faits accessoires, indifférens en apparence, et dont rien encore n'explique le retour."—p. 9.

tistical purposes, he divides France into five regions, each consisting of seventeen adjoining departments, not arbitrarily grouped together, but according to their geographical position, and which he distinguishes as the *north, south, east, west,* and *centre.**

This geometrical arrangement of the departments is very advantageous for the comparison of facts, which must be studied in masses, and it is adhered to by M. Guerry, as a basis throughout his work. Another general distinction to be kept in mind is, the division of crimes into two classes, according as they are directed against the *person*, or against *property*.

If now we represent the whole number of crimes committed in one year in France by 100, their distribution among the five regions is shown by the following table.

No. 1. A. *Crimes against the Person.*

Years	1825	1826	1827	1828	1829	1830	Mean
North	25	24	23	26	25	24	25
South	28	26	22	23	25	23	24
East	17	21	19	20	19	19	19
West	18	16	21	17	17	16	18
Centre	12	13	15	14	14	18	14
	100	100	100	100	100	100	100

B. *Crimes against Property.*

Years	1825	1826	1827	1828	1829	1830	Mean
North	41	42	42	43	44	44	42
South	12	11	11	12	12	11	12
East	18	16	17	16	14	15	16
West	17	19	19	17	17	17	18
Centre	12	12	11	12	13	13	12
	100	100	100	100	100	100	100

From this table it appears that the relative proportion of crimes committed in either of the five regions does not vary on the average of six years (1825-30), more than 1-25 part for crimes against the person, and not more than 1-50 part for crimes against property. Thus, strange as it may appear, it is certain, says M. Guerry, "que le produit annuel des récoltes

* The population of these five regions (1830) is stated as follows :—

North	8,757,700
South	4,826,493
East	5,840,996
West	7,008,788
Centre	5,238,905
	31,672,882
Corsica	185,079
Total	31,857,961

ou des impôts, dans les diverses parties du royaume, ne saurait être évalué d'avance avec plus de précision, de certitude que le nombre des vols, des meurtres, et des assassinats."

Sex.—Of every 100 persons charged annually with *theft* throughout France, the proportions of delinquents according to *sex*, are as follow.

No. 2. A. *Sex of those accused of Theft.*

Years	1826	1827	1828	1829	1830	Mean
Men	79	79	78	77	78	78
Women	21	21	22	23	22	22
	100	100	100	100	100	100

Thus the proportion of thefts committed by criminals of *different sexes* is constant within 2-100.

Age.—Of every 100 Persons accused of theft, the criminals classified by their *age* stand thus:

B. *Age of those accused of Theft.*

Of 100 criminals	1826	1827	1828	1829	1830	Mean
Age from 16 to 25 years	37	35	38	37	37	37
25 to 35 years	31	32	30	31	32	31
35 and upwards	32	33	32	32	31	32
	100	100	100	100	100	100

Here the greatest difference between any one year taken separately, and the average of five years, does not exceed 2-100, and is for the most part only 1-100.

Seasons.—The influence of the seasons in relation to some particular crimes, is shown to be equally constant and regular, the difference in any one season not exceeding by more than 2-100 the mean of four corresponding seasons.

When we reflect on the infinite variety of circumstances which may influence the production of crime, and the external or purely personal causes that may determine its character, it is not easy to conceive how things should concur to bring about such uniform results; and that voluntary actions, when viewed in masses, should be developed in a fixed order and be included within such precise limits. The fact illustrates the distinction which an ingenious writer has alluded to (but in another sense) between *man* and what we term *mankind*. The individual, as the subject of moral responsibility, is a free agent, and his life is a constant series of phenomena, more or less voluntary; but when a number of these series are compared together, the *terms*, if we may so speak, correspond or differ in such regular order, that what was most uncertain in the individual becomes a law in the aggregate; and where all seems at first sight caprice and accident, we find fixed boundaries and uniform results.*

The following table exhibits a classification of the crimes annually committed in France (with the exception of those that come before military and naval tribunals) in the order of their relative frequency, and as committed by offenders of different sexes. On the average of six years (1825-30) the total number of crimes amounts to 7147 annually, of which, crimes against the person constitute 1865, or about 1-4 part; offences against property the remaining 3-4, or 5282.

No. 3. Crimes in the order of Frequency, &c.

(Average of six years, 1825—1830.)

A. *Crimes against the Person.*

Nature of the crime.	Annual No. of Crimes.	Proportn in 1000.	Proportion in 100 committed by Men.	Proportion in 100 committed by Women.
Murder and manslaughter	553	297	92	8
Cutting and wounding	453	243	88	12
Assaults on women and children	306	164	99	1
Crimes against the state	237	127	91	9
Infanticide	118	63	6	94
Perjury and subornation of perjury	87	47	85	15
Poisoning	40	21	55	45
Parricide	13	7	64	36
Bigamy	11	5	98	2
Other crimes against the person	47	26	56	44
Annual total..	1865	1000	Mean 86	Mean 14

B. *Crimes against Property.*

Nature of the crime.	Annual No. of Crimes.	Proportn in 1000.	Proportion in 100 committed by Men.	Proportion in 100 committed by Women.
Robbery of various kinds (not otherwise specified) } 4475	3219	610	83	17
by domestics } 4475	1043	198	60	40
on the highways } 4475	159	30	92	8
in churches } 4475	54	10	78	22
Frauds and forgery of various kinds and coining	478	91	92	8
Fraudulent bankruptcy	105	20	86	14
Incendiarism and destruction of property..	129	24	84	16
Other crimes against property	95	17	82	18
Annual total .	5282	1000	Mean 79	Mean 21

* The reflection which Schiller puts into the mouth of Wallenstein, when denying

Of the crimes against the person, it appears that 1-4 consists of assaults and bodily injuries; 1-3 of deaths by violence, (and which, coupled with suicides, amount to not less than 700 annually, or nearly 2 *per diem;)* and infanticide, perjury, poisoning, &c. fill up the list in successively decreasing proportions.

Of crimes against property, 85 in 100 consist of *thefts* of various kinds. Robberies by domestics form 1-4 of the total number of robberies: highway robbery does not amount to 1-30 of the whole. After theft come the various kinds of fraud, incendiarism, forgery, &c.

The total number of offences against property (though not the more serious kinds, nor crimes of violence) seems to have increased of late years both in France and England; but this M. G. mainly attributes to the number of relapsed criminals *(les récidives)* among the young, and to the neglect of prison discipline. There is a Gaelic saying, "It is not easy to straighten in the oak the crook that grew in the sapling;" and no proof is wanting from criminal records to convince us, that any great and decided improvement in national morals must be produced by operating on the minds and manners of the young. Unfortunately this class, when delinquents, are treated nearly as if they were grown up and hardened offenders; and from being intermingled with associates who have known more of vice than themselves, they seldom come out of prison half so corrigible as they went in. M. Guerry's reflections on this topic are very judicious and interesting, but we have not space here to exhibit them in detail.

Crimes of both classes are (as might be supposed) committed in very different proportions by offenders of different sexes. As a general result it appears that

Of every 100 crimes	against the *person*,	86	are committed by	men;
..	..	14	..	women;
..	.. *property*,	79	..	men;
..	..	21	..	women.

We must be cautious however in taking these numbers as indicative of the comparative *morality* of the sexes, on account of the great difference existing between them as to their temptations and physical ability to commit crimes: so that M. G. is led to conclude, that although on the whole we may allow a higher morality to the sex, there is in reality less disproportion in this respect than is commonly supposed.

Of crimes against the person committed by women, poisoning forms

that his destiny is in the hands of chance, may be applied as well to the community as to the individual man:

"Know that the human being's thoughts and deeds
Are not, like ocean-billows, blindly moved:
The inner world—his microcosmus—is
The deep shaft out of which they spring eternally:
They grow by certain laws, like the tree's fruit;
No juggling chance can metamorphose them."

6-100; of those committed by men, it is only 1-100 part. Infanticide constitutes 2-5 of the crimes against the person committed by women; and no crime demonstrates more vividly than this the sad perversion of the natural affections, and the intensity of emotion to which women are frequently subject.*

M. Guerry's tables illustrating the influence of *age* on the commission of crime, are very elaborate and minute; but we can only find room for the following table, which represents the proportions in which crimes (combining together those against person and property) are committed at different periods of life by the two sexes. We should observe, however, that without knowing the comparative number of persons of each sex and age living at the same time in France, (an element of the calculation which M. G. does not give us) we cannot take these numbers as accurately indicating the law of tendency towards criminal actions at different periods of life.

No. 4. *Proportion of Crime at different Ages.*

AGE OF THE CRIMINALS.	Of 1000 Crimes committed by Men.	Of 1000 Crimes committed by Women.
Below 16 years	19	14
From 16 to 21	169	135
21 to 25	162	158
25 to 30	182	185
30 to 35	144	148
35 to 40	91	117
40 to 45	76	84
45 to 50	59	66
50 to 70	98	93
	1000	1000

M. G. states that his general conclusions on this head agree perfectly with the results published by M. Quételet in his recent Essay, "*Recherches sur le penchant au Crime aux différens âges,*" and which may be thus

* Strange as it appears, M. G. notices it as an unquestionable fact, that maternal tenderness and apprehensions of their children's future troubles, sometimes lead women to commit this most unnatural crime. At the same time, nothing in their previous conduct may create the suspicion of insanity: the crime is regarded as an act of devotedness—is long dwelt upon—and at length is committed without compunction. In most cases however the unhappy mother immediately after completes the tragedy by self-destruction; leaving it scarcely doubtful that the evil propensity was the result of mental hallucination, though at the same time yielding testimony to the poet's aphorism:

"Every crime
Has, in the moment of its perpetration,
Its own avenging angel—*dark misgiving*,
An ominous sinking at the inmost heart!"

summed up. The maximum of crimes takes place in the period of life between the ages of 25 and 30. In this short term of five years, occur nearly 1-5 of the total number of crimes committed by either sex. Criminal tendencies are developed earlier in man than woman: with the first they gather comparatively greater strength between the ages of 16 and 21, and on the other hand, decline more rapidly than with women, particularly after the age of 35; but beyond the age of 50, culpable tendencies are nearly the same in both.

The influence of the *seasons* is shown in the different proportion of crimes committed in the several months and quarters of the year. We omit the table, the general result being that the greatest number of offences against the *person* are committed in summer, the smallest number in winter, spring and autumn being nearly alike;* and that with respect to crimes against *property*, these proportions are reversed, so that the maximum of one class coincides with the minimum of the other;—a fact certainly worthy of observation, as illustrating the system of compensation that prevails throughout nature. The different length of the days, rather than the variation of temperature, is considered by M. G. as the chief cause of the influence attributable to the seasons.

After some remarks on the importance of studying the Statistics of Insanity, with the view of determining if there is any connection between the greater prevalence of mental derangement, and of violent crimes at the same period of the year; M. G. proceeds to an estimate of the force of different passions and irregular habits in the production of the more serious crimes. His conclusions on this subject (which are only very partially shown by the table at foot†) are strongly confirmatory of the position which in this part of his work M. G. is led to dwell upon, viz. the coin-

* The crime of *infanticide* is more frequent in the spring and winter than in the other seasons, corresponding to the proportion of births in each period. The month of March, in which this crime is most frequent, is next to February, the month in which the greatest number of births takes place throughout the year.

† No. 5. *Apparent Motives of the Crimes of Homicide, Poisoning, and Incendiarism.*

		In 1000 crimes
I.	Hatred and revenge	264
II.	Domestic dissension	143
III.	Quarrels at play and in public places	113
IV.	To aid in or conceal theft	102
V.	Sudden broils	94
VI.	Local disputes and adverse interests	80
VII.	Adultery	64
VIII.	Debauchery	53
IX.	To secure the succession to property	26
X.	To obtain insurance premiums	25
XI.	Disappointed love and refusals of marriage	20
XII.	Jealousy	16
		1000

cidence of sound views of *utility* and *duty* as guides to our social conduct: but without going into the detail of facts which he has collected, exhibiting the evils of profligacy in its different shapes, (a task both painful in itself and here not suitable) it would be difficult to convey a sufficiently strong impression of the support which his researches furnish to the vital truth, that the rules of right and of utility are inseparable. The reporter justly characterises M. G.'s reflections on this subject as "*pleines de sagesse et de raison.*"

We come next to consider the *geographical distribution* of Crimes in France, by which we obtain a general idea of the comparative morality of different districts of the country, and are led to inquire into the causes of the diversities observed. The following table shows with reference both to crimes against the person and against property, the proportion of crimes to the population in each of the five regions, upon the average of six years, from 1825 to 1830 inclusive.

No. 6. *Crime and Instruction.*

REGIONS.	Accused of crimes against		Proportion of Scholars of male sex in 1829. (Inhabitants.)
	Persons.	Property.	
South	1 in 11,003	1 in 7,945	1 in 43
East	.. 17,349	.. 6,949	.. 14
North	.. 19,964	.. 3,924	.. 16
Centre	.. 20,984	.. 8,285	.. 48
West	. 22,168	.. 7,534	.. 45
Mean of all France..	1 in 17,085	1 in 6,031	1 in 38

From this table it appears that great disparity exists between different parts of the country, so far as their morality can be estimated by the proportion of crimes in each. Of the five regions, the *south* is that in which the greatest number of crimes against the *person* are committed relatively to the population. Next comes the *east*, then the *north*, *centre*, and *west*. In the two latter regions, these crimes are scarcely half so frequent in proportion to the population, as in the south. On comparing the departments individually, the difference is still greater; those of *Corsica* and *Creuse* being at the two extremes of the scale. In the first, there is one charge of crime against the person to every 2199 inhabitants; in the latter (Creuse), only one in 37,014, or in a ratio fifteen times more favourable than in Corsica. The mean for the whole of France is one accused to 17,085 of the population. Thirty-one departments present an average more favourable than this; the remaining 55 in different degrees exceed it. M. G. states in a table the numerical proportion for each department.

The relative position of the five regions, and of most of the departments individually, is different with respect to crimes against *property*, as will be seen by the table. This class of crimes is most numerous relatively to the population in the *north*, next in the *east*, and the *west*, *south*, *centre*, follow in this order. In the latter region, these crimes are not half so frequent as in the north, in proportion to the population.

Among the *departments*, that of the Seine, in which the capital is situated, ranks first, as might be expected, in the scale of crimes against *property*; there being one accused to 1368 inhabitants. In *Creuse*, which exhibits an equally favourable morality in regard to this as to the other class of crimes, there is only one accused to 20,235 inhabitants. The mean for the whole kingdom is one to 6031 : 62 departments present more favourable proportions than the mean, 24 are above it.

The distribution of the two classes of crimes is in general such, that by a happy compensation, those parts of the kingdom which shew the greatest number of crimes against the person are least fruitful in offences against property. There is an exception, however, in prejudice of the departments of Corsica, Seine-et-Oise, Mozelle, and Lozère, which stand unfortunately high in both scales.

M. G. enters at some length into the consideration of the causes which most materially influence the varied prevalence of crimes of each class. He sees reason to attribute the marked distinction in the distribution of crimes against the *person*, chiefly to differences of generic character among the tribes that constitute the population of France; all of whom still retain to a certain extent their own languages, customs, and traditional prejudices. The inhabitants of the south, where these crimes most abound, differ considerably in race and organisation from the inhabitants of other parts of France. The livelier sensibility and hastiness of temper which characterize them, give rise to numerous disputes and broils; and the passions of jealousy and revenge are not unfrequently evidenced in personal outrages among them.

With respect to the distribution of crimes against *property*, their apparent connection with the advancement of commerce and industry affords ground for very instructive inquiry. The question of the influence of wealth and poverty on national morals is one of the most intricate that Statistics can be brought to elucidate : but as yet we are in want of documents sufficiently authentic to deserve much attention. It must not be forgotten, in considering the influence of other causes on the amount of crime, that the absolute amount of wealth in a district is far from being an accurate index to the condition of the great bulk of the population. The recent researches indeed of M. de Villeneuve Bargemont fully confirm M. G.'s supposition, that the pauperised districts in France, as in other countries, are precisely those in which at the same time wealth is most abundant.* Hence, the destitution and misery prevailing in a district where

* In the northern region, the chief seat of the cotton manufactories of France,

riches and civilization are rapidly increasing, may, for a time at least, completely check and nullify all the ameliorating influences that are simultaneously in operation.

M. G. exhibits a coloured chart and tables, illustrating the distribution of illegitimate births throughout France, as calculated by M. Villermé: but into the details we shall not here enter. The facts, however, which he has collected, lead him to express a decided opinion on the evils of such institutions as foundling hospitals, which sacrifice at the shrine of charity some of the strongest safeguards of the severer virtues: a case to which the reporter of the committee finds a parallel in the operation of the English Poor Laws, as he remarks, "C'est ainsi qu'en Angleterre la charité légale accroît indéfiniment le nombre des pauvres."*

Public Charities.

The degree in which the benevolent dispositions are manifested among any people, in the shape of public charities, constitutes an interesting feature in their moral character and condition: but the documents on this subject are too generally defective to afford any satisfactory conclusions. France however presents the best field for such inquiries, in consequence of the legal regulations under which all appropriations to religious or benevolent establishments must be made. For every such appropriation exceeding the sum of 300 francs (£12), a "royal ordinance of authorisation" is necessary: these ordinances are registered and inserted in the "Bulletin des Loix."

pauperism is as prevalent as in the worst regulated parts of England; every sixth inhabitant being dependent wholly or in part on charitable funds. In Creuse, a central department, and which exhibits the smallest proportion of crimes against person and property, but which presents such an aspect of poverty as to have been termed the Connaught of France, only 1-58 of the people are classed as paupers. These facts (says an intelligent journalist) "prove that, though the proportion is not every where exactly preserved, yet pauperism seems generally to increase with wealth and civilization:" and it is important to bear this tendency in mind, in considering the influence of instruction on the state of crime.—Economie Politique Chrétienne, &c. par M. le Vicomte A. de Villeneuve Bargemont: Paris, 1834.

* In the face of this obvious truth, what an outcry—disgraceful to the manly reason of the age—has been raised against that excellent measure, the Poor Laws Amendment Act! Its results however will soon convince the most inveterate gainsayers, that the system of indiscriminate relief is not that which best consults either the comfort or the morality of the poor. In a letter dated March, 1830, Mr. Coleridge has left on record a valuable testimony to this effect, which may fairly be opposed to the dolorous vaticinations of his later days, when declaiming against the new Poor Law arrangements: "It would be most unchristian moroseness not to feel delight in the unwearied zeal with which every mode and direction of charity is supported; and I hope that this is a sun-shiny spot in our national character.... *But it would on the other hand be wilful blindness not to see that the lower orders become more and more improvident in consequence, and more and more exchange the sentiments of Englishmen for the feelings of Lazzaroni.*"—Letters, &c. i. 27.

M. G. exhibits the results of his investigation under the three heads of

1. Gifts and bequests to the poor;
2. .. to the clergy and religious establishments;
3. .. to schools.

His calculations are founded solely on the number of such donations, without regard to their value, for reasons which he satisfactorily explains.

1. Of the total number of gifts and bequests, more than half, or 52 in 100, are made in favour of the poor, hospitals, &c.; and of these about 3-5 by men, 2-5 by women. Anonymous donors to the poor are in the proportion of 1 to 16. Of donors to the clergy, only 1 in 49 conceals his name. About double the amount is bequeathed to the poor, of that which is legally transferred for their use, *the donors still living*; and a curious diversity occurs in the proportions in which charity is bestowed by women, in different states of life, as shown by the table at foot.*

There is a decided preponderance of charitable offerings in the south-eastern departments of France, as compared with the others; the smallest number being shared by the central and western provinces.

With a slight exception, it appears that in those departments where the Catholic clergy are most numerous, and which at the same time present the highest proportion of crimes against the person, and of illegitimate births, the greatest benevolence is manifested towards the poor, both in gifts and bequests. In this coincidence, M. G. traces the influence of the peculiar manners and character, which distinguish in so many other respects the inhabitants of the south of France.

Those departments in which public instruction is least diffused, are also the most scanty in their benefactions to the *clergy*, still more so to the *poor*.

2. Benefactions to the clergy and religious establishments constitute nearly a moiety of the total number. The larger proportion of these are contributed by men, though the contrary has often been affirmed. M. G. corrects a popular error, that the clergy receive more by legacies than in benefactions from the living, the fact being otherwise.

The same rule obtains in respect to this as to the former class of benefactions, when made by women. By contributions during life, married women give more than spinsters, and the latter than widows: in their *bequests* the order is reversed. (See table No. 7.)

* No. 7. *Benefactions by Women.*

CLASSES.	To the Poor.		To Religious Establishments.	
	Gifts.	Bequests.	Gifts.	Bequests.
Married Women .	38	25	41	24
Unmarried......	33	36	31	38
Widows	29	39	28	38
	100	100	100	100

The benefactions to *Protestant* establishments bear a very small ratio to the total number, not more than 1 in 150. But, although the Protestants give less in proportion than the Catholics to the poor, they not unfrequently lend support to the Catholic institutions as well as to their own, and their benefactions to schools are proportionally the most numerous.

With the slight exception offered by some departments of Brittany and the south, it is in those parts of the kingdom which are most rich and enlightened, and which have long been distinguished by their liberal elections and industry, that we find the greatest number of benefactions towards *religious establishments.*

3. *Schools.* Donations for the support of public schools are in France the rarest of all. They do not exceed 1-30 of the total number of benefactions, whilst in England, says M. Guerry, where such aid is less necessary, (?) they constitute 1-3 of the whole.

Schools, like the clergy, receive more from living benefactors than in bequests, and more from men than women. Whether by donations in life time or by legacies, spinsters are found to give more to schools than married women or widows.

Anonymous donors to schools are proportionally five times more numerous, than among benefactors to the clergy. In the north-eastern departments of France, where it is well known instruction most prevails, the donations to schools are most numerous, particularly in Franche-Comtè, and Normandy.

There are 17 departments in which, during a period of *ten years,* not a single bequest has been made in favour of schools. Thirteen of these are in the western and central divisions, and eleven of them lie contiguous to each other. Throughout all of them, it is almost unnecessary to add, instruction is at its lowest pitch.

A few departments in the north-west and south may stand comparison with the most enlightened districts in their support of schools. This favourable result M. Guerry ascribes in part to the *statistical account* published some years since, of the neglected state of primary instruction in those parts of the kingdom, by which a stimulus has been given to efforts of amelioration.*

Suicides.

For some time past, Suicide has ceased to be considered as a fit subject

* It would be a curious inquiry, and probably productive of many useful results, to follow out the idea suggested by the following statement of Mr. Simpson's: "The *entire generation* is apt to take credit for the institutions of charity. The subscription lists tell a different tale. It has been observed, that about 1500 *known* individuals, of the 150,000 of which Edinburgh is composed, support all the charitable establishments of the place. The London proportion would be 15,000. It would be interesting to know how the fact stands,—*charity* balls and musical festivals of course excluded."—On Pop. Educ. p. 56.

for legislative interference in France; but it is not the less a matter of deep interest to the moralist and the statesman, to be furnished with accurate details relative to this species of moral malady;—a malady so fatal, as to snatch from their families and country almost 2000 individuals every year, the greater part of whom are in the flower of their age.

It is a duty seriously incumbent on the superior government, to collect the facts, and publish periodical statements on this subject. By the official returns, the number of suicides throughout France in the four years 1827-1830 amounted to 6900, or nearly 1800 annually; but M. G. considers it out of doubt that the suicides actually committed are nearly double this number. But, taking even the lowest estimate, which is at least treble the number of *murders* committed in a like period, it would appear that when a death occurs in France from violence, (excluding accidents and involuntary homicides) the probability is as 3 to 1 that the victim has fallen by his own hand, rather than by the hand of another.

The *geographical distribution* of suicides is not less regular than that of other crimes, both against person and property; as is shewn by the following table.

No. 8. *Suicides.*

REGIONS.	1827	1828	1829	1830	Mean Number in 100.	Proportion of Suicides to Population.
North ..	51 ..	48 ..	54 ..	51	51	1 to 9,853 Inhabitants.
East....	17 ..	16 ..	15 ..	14	16	.. 21,734
South...	14 ..	15 ..	12 ..	12	13	.. 30,499
West...	11 ..	11 ..	11 ..	11	11	.. 30,876
Centre..	9 ..	10 ..	8 ..	10	9	.. 27,393
	100	100	100	100	100	
	Mean of all France..				.. ..	1 to 18,320

It will be seen from this table that during these four years, the annual proportion of suicides in either region has not varied more than 3-100 from the mean. In the centre, the variation has not exceeded 1-100; and in the west the proportion for each of the fourteen years is uniform.

The different regions do not stand quite in the same order, as to their proportions of suicides absolutely taken, as when these are compared with their respective population; but in either case, the northern departments are sadly distinguished by an excessive number. Next follows the east, then the centre, south, and west. In the two latter regions, suicides are in general thrice as rare as in the north.

The disproportion among the departments individually, is still more striking. Thus, in that of the Seine, the suicides are as 1 to 3500 inhabitants; in the Higher Pyrenees, only as 1 to 220,000. Between these extremes, range the other 84 departments; the mean for the whole of France is as 1 to 18,320 of the population. There are 27 departments in which the proportion is greater; 59 in which it is less.

The department of the Seine, comprising the capital, in which 1-6 of the illegitimate births occur, exhibits a similar proportion in respect to suicides. In this one department there occur as many suicides as in 32 departments of the south and centre.

As a general fact, it is very remarkable that in the line of approach to Paris from every quarter, the number of suicides regularly increases as we get nearer to the capital. Something of the same kind is observed in the vicinity of Marseilles, which seems to stand relatively to Provence and Dauphiny, in much the same position as Paris to the rest of France.*

The mixture of rudeness and irascibility, which in the southern provinces causes so many sudden broils, might be supposed to favour the commission of suicide. Facts, however, prove that the departments in which personal outrages are most frequent, are exactly those in which suicides are the fewest, and *vice versâ.*

M. G. offers some interesting reflections on the predominating motives to suicide, and suggests an analysis of the papers so generally left by the unhappy victims, as a means of estimating the relative frequency or degree of activity of the causes of self-murder. He gives a sketch of such an analysis of 100 documents in the archives of the Prefecture of Police, but we cannot enter into the details. One of the inducements to suicide recorded in his table, appears not a little singular,—*the desire to obtain the prayers of the church:* but apparent inconsistencies of this kind are more frequent than we might anticipate. Many suicides sign themselves with the cross before terminating their existence; others throw themselves on their knees and make their prayers, or adorn themselves with beads, and peruse books of devotion.

Though nothing can appear more accidental and uncertain than the *mode* that will be chosen by a person about to terminate his life, it will be

* As about 1-3 of the population of Paris consists of *strangers*, it is interesting to know in what proportions the natives and inhabitants of the different departments become suicides *in that city*. A curious table is given by M. G. to elucidate this point, and it is remarkable that of 1000 suicides in Paris, the proportions for the 12 departments which rank first in the *Parisian* list, nearly correspond with those assigned to them when compared with the country at large. The distribution of *Parisian* suicides among the *five regions* gives a still more striking result. Of 1000 suicides committed in Paris, there belong to the

North	505
East	210
Centre	168
West	65
South	52
	1000

In this table the five regions maintain the same order (excepting only the transposition of the west and south) as in the general table, No. 8, for the whole kingdom. The northern region (after taking out the department of the Seine) still produces more than half the total number.

found that chance has no more operation in this case than in the distribution of crimes, or the other general facts of Statistics. The choice is influenced by age, sex, social condition, and a multitude of other circumstances very difficult to distinguish, but very traceable in the constancy of their results.*

On the average of suicides occurring at any given period of life, it is found that choice is made of one mode of destruction in a very marked degree of preference to others. Thus, in youth, says M. G. a man hangs himself; in maturer age recourse is had to a deadly weapon; and as his vigour declines, the first means again come into favour, and it is generally by suspension that an old man puts an end to life. These results are illustrated by the table at foot;† and the more numerous, says M. Guerry, are our observations on this subject, the greater we shall find the constancy of the proportions given.

INSTRUCTION.

Having thus presented more or less in detail the facts and inferences which M. G. furnishes on the other subjects comprised in the department of "Moral Statistics," we come now, and in the last place, to a review of the Statistics of *Instruction* in France. The basis on which our author's calculations are founded requires specific notice. In 1823 public attention in France was directed by the illustrious geographer M. Malte Brun, to the remarkable difference in respect to instruction, between different parts of the kingdom, whence arose the distinction of "*La France obscure*," and "*La France éclairée*." We are indebted, however, for the first statistical documents on this subject, to the learned Venetian geographer M. Balbi, published in his work, "Statistique du Royaume de Portugal et d'Algarve." The only basis of calculation then possessed, or which has been used by later inquirers, (except M. Guerry) was the number of pupils of the male sex admitted into the public schools. But M. G. thinks

* "When we pass from individuals to masses, we find even in those actions which seem most fortuitous, a regularity of production, an order of succession, that can only arise from fixity of cause."—For. Quar. Rev. xvi. 213.

† No. 9. *Suicides.*

AGE OF VICTIMS.	Of 1000 Suicides By Pistol.	By Hanging.
From 10 to 20 years..	61	68
20 to 30	283	51
30 to 40	182	94
40 to 50	150	188
50 to 60	161	256
60 to 70	126	235
Above 70	37	108
	1000	1000

that the distribution of instruction can now be determined from better data. Since 1827, the Minister of War has subjected all the young men drawn for the army to an examination, which shows the number of those who can read and write at the period of their being drawn. Taking these results for three years as a basis, M. G. has constructed tables exhibiting the relative state of instruction in the different departments. If to illustrate the same facts, we take a map of France, and shade it in proportion to the scantiness of instruction, we shall find a strong line of demarcation between the northern and southern provinces. When the line is drawn from La Manche in the north-west, to the department of the Jura in the east, it will be found that an almost uniform light tint overspreads twenty departments in the northern part of the kingdom. The most favourable proportion in this division is presented by the department of the *Meuse*, in which 74 out of 100 conscripts can *read and write*; and the lowest proportion in this division is found in the "département du Nord," where only 45 out of 100 conscripts are equally advanced.

The southern provinces are not (as has been supposed) those in which ignorance most prevails, but rather the provinces of the west and centre, Berry, Limousin, and Brittany. In the department of Finisterre, only 15 out of 100 conscripts could read and write, in Morbihan 14, and in Corrèze only 12,—this department being the lowest of all in the scale.

In five departments of the west the amount of instruction is above the average of the kingdom. In Corsica, where ignorance has been supposed greatly to prevail, about half of the youthful conscripts can read and write. In 60 departments the average is below this.

The average amount of instruction throughout the 86 departments is expressed by the proportion of 38 out of 100 conscripts, able to *read and write*. There are 44 departments above this mean, 42 below it.

Taking the facts as M. G. has stated them, we have now to advert to his views on the important question, "How far is the state of *crime* influenced by the state of *instruction*?" No question can be more interesting to the philanthropist, none more important to the legislator. Whatever *à priori* opinions we may entertain, it is not the less necessary we should attend to the evidence of *facts*. In this way only shall we acquire an energetic conviction of the utility of our labours, or find a safeguard against undue confidence in certain processes and machinery, which may delude us under the fair name of being that which *it really is not*.

Some of M. G.'s conclusions on this subject are opposed to what is now both the popular and (we hope to show) the only correct opinion: but we must not give the less credit to his principles or love of truth, because a more extended comparison of facts may lead us to differ from him.

In proof of the position that ignorance is the principal cause of crime, it is asserted that the departments in which instruction is least diffused, are those in which most crimes are committed. But M. Guerry joins issue on the *fact*. On examining the condition of the several departments, it appears that the maximum amount of crimes against the *person* is found in Corsica, in the provinces of the south-east, and in Alsace. But it is *not* in these parts that ignorance is most prevalent. On the other hand, the minimum of this class of crimes is found in the western and central provinces, where certainly instruction is not the most diffused. With respect to offences against *property*, M. G. considers it unnecessary to institute a similar comparison, as this class of crimes is confessedly most prevalent in the best instructed districts; and for a long time past it has been admitted that these crimes should not be attributed chiefly to ignorance, as it has been customary to do.

From an examination of the official records, our author is led to believe that a larger proportion of the crimes against the *person* than of those against *property*, are committed by parties who have received instruction. Again, the proportion of those brought to trial who are unable to read, proves nothing as to the effect of ignorance, unless we can show that the bulk of the population, of which these criminals form part, is in a more advanced state of instruction.* Nor does there appear sufficient evidence for concluding that the ratio of *youthful* convicts has progressively decreased, as instruction has been diffused.

"All these results, unexpected as they are," says M. Guerry, "were not our researches limited to France, we could show to agree with those obtained by men of great probity and intelligence, who have instituted inquiries in the most enlightened communities. In England, in Germany, and in the United States, where some years since all was congratulation on the happy influence of instruction and industry on moral advancement; it is now admitted that to found schools is not enough to check demoralization, and that some other remedy must be sought to extirpate the evils that oppress society."†

* "We are always told that the majority of criminals cannot *read*, as if the mere faculty of reading would have diminished the number of criminals.... But if the investigation had gone the length of ascertaining with which of the criminals had an attempt at moral training and useful knowledge ever been made, we should have found *that* column of the table a blank, and something like cause and effect would begin to dawn upon us."—Simpson, p. 35.

† This reference to the experience of the United States is supported by a communication made to M. Guerry by M. M. G. de Beaumont and A. de Tocqueville, two magistrates of the Royal Court of Paris, whose attention during a visit to North America was particularly given to the working of the penitentiary system, and the general state of crime. Their work, "*Du Système Pénitentiare des Etats Unis,*" which at the time M. G. wrote was unpublished, has since been given to the world, and has conferred a high character for intelligence and fairness on its authors. After noticing the care of the state governments of New York and Connecticut to spread education, notwithstanding which (in the latter state particularly) crimes have continued to increase with extreme rapidity, M. M. Beaumont and De Tocqueville acknowledge that if this increased prevalence of crime is not to be attributed to the

"Perhaps," adds M. G. in the true spirit of a philosopher, "we shall be reproached with overturning theories of long standing, and consecrated by the most respectable authority. Our reply is, that we are not concerned with any *theory (nous ne faisons point de doctrine)*:—our task is to bring forward *facts* without professing to explain them. We are also fully convinced that every error cannot but be ultimately pernicious; and that if we would advance science, or benefit our fellow-men, we must bend the authority of names to that of facts, and never sacrifice to secondary considerations what bears the character of a truth."

"Are we to conclude," he next asks, "from the foregoing remarks, that the cultivation of the intellect, instead of weakening criminal propensities, tends rather to strengthen them? This would be to fall into a new error."

"Knowledge, properly considered, is a mere instrument, of which either a good or a bad use may be made. Such as is given in our elementary schools, and is limited to an imperfect acquisition of the arts of reading and writing, cannot supply the place of *education*, and seems quite unfit to exercise much influence on the moral character. The correct opinion seems to be, that it renders the pupil neither better nor worse; for it is not easy to understand how the training a child to certain almost mechanical operations, can possibly in itself be the means of giving him correct habits, or of developing in him sentiments of honour and probity."

With these views, however, our author is far from representing such elementary knowledge as without its use, and he attributes much praise to those honourable and disinterested men,

"*Statists* indeed and lovers of their country,"

who during the last fifteen years have been endeavouring to diffuse it.

diffusion of knowledge, we are yet compelled to admit that this has not sufficed to repress crime. Their concluding reflections I will offer in their own words: "Instruction," say they, "even when comprising religious belief, gives birth to a multitude of new desires, which, unsatisfied, may lead those who experience them into crime. Knowledge multiplies the social relations: it is the soul of commerce and of industry; but thus it creates also a thousand occasions of fraud, which do not exist among a rude and ignorant people. The tendency of instruction is therefore rather to increase than to diminish the number of crimes. In the present day this result is generally admitted, for we find in Europe that crimes are progressive in most of the countries where instruction is most diffused. On the other hand," say these gentlemen, "we will take this occasion to give a complete idea of what we think of the influence of instruction. Its advantages appear to us infinitely to outweigh its inconveniences. It stimulates every variety of intellect, and lends support to all the industrial arts. It thus gives security to the moral sentiments and the material well-being of a people. The passions which it excites, though injurious to society when unable to find objects to satisfy them, become pregnant with advantages when they can attain their desired ends. Thus instruction, it is true, may scatter some seeds of corruption among men; but it is that also which advances a people in wealth and strength. And in a community surrounded by enlightened nations, it is not only a benefit, but even a necessity of state."—Du Syst. Pénitent. par. 1, ch. iii.

"If the instruction," he concludes, "hitherto attempted has not produced all the benefits anticipated, it has at least destroyed many absurd and injurious prejudices; it has given some orderly habits; it has favoured the application of the working classes to the less onerous employments, and has thus tended to mitigate and improve their social condition."

We have preferred presenting M. Guerry's views on this important topic in a complete state, that no one may conclude from his strict adherence to the guidance of facts, that he is opposed to the cause of public education.* It is proper however to state some circumstances which tend to modify the conclusions adopted by our author, respecting the influence of instruction on crime, and which may be found more in detail in an article in the "Companion to the British Almanac for 1835" (p. 53). M. G.'s data then we must observe, show but imperfectly the intellectual condition of the *whole people*, inasmuch as they tell us nothing respecting the state of instruction of females, as they include only young men of the ages at which they are liable to be drawn for the army; and above all, as no distinction is shown in the returns made to the Minister of War, of the number of conscripts who have received instruction *beyond* reading and writing. Now it is shown very satisfactorily in the Essay just referred to, that the average number of *convictions* among the *instructed class* being 1592 annually, (which is rather a smaller number than M. G.'s ratio of 38 instructed to 100 inhabitants should produce) the proportions in which these 1592 had enjoyed the different degrees of instruction stand thus:

No. 10. *Instructed Convicts.*

STATE OF INSTRUCTION.	Number Convicted.	Proportion in 100.	Proportion to whole Popul.ⁿ (32,561,463)
Able to read *or* write imperfectly ..	1140	72	1 to 28,562
.. *and* .. well	388	24	.. 83,921
Instructed beyond reading and writing	64	4	.. 508,773
	1592	100	1 to 20,453 Mean

As the proportion of the *convicted* to the *committals* is smaller among the better *instructed* criminals, it is evident that so far the basis on which M. G. calculates the distribution of crime, viz. the number of the *accused*, is unfavourable to an exact estimate of the influence of instruction. Again, when we examine the intellectual condition of persons accused as *relapsed*

* "This opposition comes of the imperfection of the education of those who show it;—an imperfection that has other bitter fruits. The only excuse for it is the ignorance of these opinionists of the length, and breadth, and height, and depth, of the social error which they ['by incogitate habit'] espouse and circulate."—Simpson, p. 37.

criminals, the result is decidedly in favour of the good tendency of instruction. On the average of four years, 1829 to 1832, the annual number of relapsed criminals amounts to 1357, who are distributed into four classes, as follows :

No. 11. *Relapsed Criminals (Les Récidives).*

CLASSES.	Number Accused.	Number Acquitted.	Per Cent.
Wholly uninstructed	836	168 or	$20\frac{1}{10}$
Able to read *or* write imperfectly	374	85 ..	$22\frac{7}{10}$
.. *and* .. well............	125	36 ..	$28\frac{8}{10}$
Instructed beyond reading and writing ..	22	9 ..	$41\frac{3}{10}$
	1357	298	22 Mean

As the proportion of relapsed criminals who were *acquitted* in each class, increases with their degree of information, it seems to be proved that however overcome for a time by the force of temptation, instruction *has* a tendency to make the experience of punishment profitable to the offender.

In comparing the several Departments as to the number of criminals which they furnish, and the degree of instruction which they have received, we must bear in mind the wide diversities of character in the inhabitants of the different provinces, which must materially affect their susceptibility of the influence of education, so far at least as certain crimes and propensities are concerned. But it appears even from M. G.'s data, that if instruction has not invariably a marked effect in the repression of crime, yet that it cannot be visited with the reproach of disposing men to criminal acts. The writer of the article already referred to,* after contrasting together four of the *most* with four of the *least* enlightened departments, from the two extremes of the scale, and showing that in the latter where instruction is most neglected, crime is by no means least prevalent, (and so reciprocally in the other four) justly concludes :

"It is here seen that not only is the proportion of criminals to the entire population smallest in the best-instructed districts, but the nature of the crimes committed is less serious :—a result which cannot fail to prove satisfactory to those who look to the cultivation of the minds of their fellow-citizens, as to the surest means of redeeming them from vicious habits."†

* Companion to the Almanac, *ut supra.*

† These remarks are so fully confirmed by Mr. W. R. Greg's valuable "Report on the Social Statistics of the Netherlands," (read at the last meeting of the British Association in Dublin) and his conclusions are altogether so important, that it would be unpardonable to omit giving them in detail. The following table relates to the

It is quite true that these results do not invalidate M. G.'s proofs that on a comparison of larger districts, their moral condition does not correspond very closely to the degree in which they enjoy elementary instruction. But on the other hand, were we even to admit, as M. M. Beaumont and De Tocqueville say, "that it is in the nature of instruction rather to increase than to diminish the number of crimes," we should be justified in looking upon this as only a temporary and incidental consequence. The balance of good would still remain on the other side: nor are we to regard the

kingdom of the Netherlands, which Mr. Greg divides statistically into four divisions according to the degree of instruction in each:—

DISTRICTS.	Per Centage of the Popul^n at Schools.	One Murder, Rape, or Violent Assault to Inhabitants.
In the 5 first provinces where ..	13.9	52.960
.. 5 next	11.5	43.380
.. 5 next	10.3	31.700
.. 4 last	7.9	20.720

"Thus we *do* find," adds Mr. Greg, "that where the greatest quantum of education exists, the more heinous crimes of violence diminish in frequency. Upon crimes of *fraud* I should doubt any effect being produced, (appreciable by similar tables) as the causes of these depend often less on the individual, if we may so speak, than on the circumstances by which he is surrounded.

"The fairest and most satisfactory mode however of ascertaining the effect of education in diminishing crime, is to ascertain *the proportion of offenders* who have received instruction. M. Guerry thinks that even in this way no accurate or gratifying result can be arrived at. Let us examine the state of matters in France, Belgium, and America. The data for constructing the following table are taken from M. Quételet and Dr. Lieber, and reduced to centesimal proportions.

Degree of Education of Criminals.	In 1000 Crimes in France against Property.	In 1000 Crimes in France against Person.	Crimes agst Per^n to Crimes agst Prop^y comm^d by each class, as 1 to	In 1000 of all kinds of crimes in France.	In 1000 of all kinds of crimes in Belgium.	In 1000 of all kinds of crimes in America.
None	616	583	3.2	610	610	256
Very imperfect..	262	282	2.8	266	150	551
Decent	103	113	2.7	103	200	180
Superior	19	22	2.6	21	40	13
	1000	1000	..	1000	1000	1000

"Two conclusions are to be drawn from this table which has been constructed with the greatest care.

"1. That 81 *per cent.* of the crimes are committed by persons having received no education, or a very imperfect one; and only 19 *per cent.* by those having had the benefit of a decent or a superior one.

"2. That the best educated commit *proportionally* more crimes of violence than of fraud. This is natural, inasmuch as while their passions are equally strong, their temptations to theft are incomparably less than those of the ignorant, who are generally also the poor. Nor must this be considered as in any way contradicting the last table. The two combined prove:—1. That crimes of violence diminish in proportion as education increases. And 2. That crimes of fraud diminish in a still more rapid ratio."—Report, &c. pp. 26, 27.

partial evils of popular instruction as the only ill effects attributable to mental culture and the progress of civilization, which nevertheless are accounted blessings by every sane mind.*

From some of his remarks already quoted, it is evident that M. G. is aware with what caution the inferences resulting from the existing state of *instruction* are to be extended to the influence of what is rightly termed *education.* He alludes to the general oversight of the wide difference which exists in the kind of mental culture respectively indicated by these terms; a distinction however which has not escaped notice by some of the most eminent of the French publicists. In a lecture delivered in 1817, M. Royer Collard strongly insists upon it in these words: "Sans l'éducation, l'instruction ne serait qu'un instrument de ruine....Les mœurs naissent de l'éducation, l'éducation seule les crée et les perpétue, parceque seule elle enseigne véritablement le devoir *en le réduisant en pratique.*"

These remarks give us a clue to much of the contrariety of opinion prevalent on this subject, both in France and our own country. The idea is too absurd to merit formal refutation, that a creature endowed with the faculties of *man*, is intended to find his happiness and welfare in the neglect of that very portion of his nature which marks his superiority to other animated beings.† It is in fact nothing less than a libel on the Divine wisdom, to suppose that there breathes one human being gifted with understanding, conscience, and will, to whom education must not be an invaluable blessing. But then comes the momentous enquiry what *is* education? Is it the mere acquisition by rote of certain facts or moral lessons, whilst the intellect is unexercised, and the habits undisciplined? Or on the other hand, is it the infusion of knowledge and cultivation of the reasoning powers, to the neglect of the moral affections of our nature and of the sense of *responsibility*, which is the cement of human society? Either of these methods may be called *instruction* as respects certain powers and portions of our nature; but to neither of them singly should we apply the term *education*, which is not a partial and incomplete work, but has reference to

* It is a fact admitted by most writers on insanity, (and particularly noticed in Dr. Prichard's admirable work) that *mental disease* is comparatively rare among *savage* nations, and even unknown among some tribes. "It comes forward," says the Dr. "with the dawning of civilization, and perhaps keeps pace, though its increase is modified by other circumstances, with the advancement of mental cultivation." M. Pariset, an able and eloquent writer on this subject, (quoted by Dr. P.) carries his opinion still further, but justly concludes in words equally applicable to the incidental evils of popular education,—"The more there is of liberty in any country, the more numerous are the chances of derangement; but this does not prevent our allowing that liberty is favourable also to the expansion of human reason."—Prichard on Insanity, pp. 340, 351.

† "The animals are guided aright by their instincts: man ought to be directed as truly by his observing and reflecting powers, which were given him for that end; but then the condition of cultivation and improvement was annexed to the gift, and that command of the All-wise is forgotten and disobeyed."—Simpson, p. 13.

all the faculties and affections of the mind, and must *bring out* the *whole man* into the full and efficient exercise of his capacities and duties.* As virtue then consists not merely in a knowledge of what is right, but in a corresponding habit of action, we must not look for disproportionate results when instruction is confined to the arts of reading and writing. "A book," says a judicious writer,† "informs us what habits ought to be—right education insures a number of *acts* in accordance with the principle laid down in the book." Rote learning can never reach the active principles that govern the conduct, or the teaching of texts and rules be an effectual substitute for *moral training*, education's paramount object. No system in short can fulfil the design of a sound education, which, while it inculcates the acquisition of knowledge and the exercise of the intellect, does not aim also at bringing the moral nature (as Sir James Mackintosh has beautifully said) "to look on the understanding itself as something that is only the first of its instruments." The whole constitution of nature, and its admirable adaptation to the faculties of man as a moral, intelligent, and religious being, point to the conclusion that rectitude is the only way of securing happiness. If this is truth for the individual, it is no less truth for the community, and it should be the polar star of all efforts for social amelioration. The finest state machinery must be subject to derangement, unless the parts are so shapen and proportioned as to work harmoniously, and with a due dependence on each other. Overlooking this truth, many patriotic and enlightened men, in whose view the political constitution of a country was every thing, have seen their labours end in failure and disappointment. Their minds in fact have forerun their age, and over-rated the materials with which they had to work, forgetful of the principle, so well stated by an able writer,‡ that "no political arrangements can transmute the effects of ignorance into those of knowledge; or bring it to pass that an unenlightened people can be as well governed under free institutions as an enlightened one."§

* "A plan of education may be devised which shall be admirably adapted for opening and invigorating the *intellect*, when viewed in itself. But how shall we get it to be acted on? How shall we ensure the development of the intellect, unless we interest also those feelings which, in the complex being man, are inseparably combined with the intellectual powers? since it is not reason that thinks and judges and infers, but reasoning man;—not the abstract principle of intellect, but intellect as it physically exists, and as it is modified and controlled by our active and sensitive nature."—Dr. Hampden, Lect. on Mor. Phil. p. 60.

† Quarterly Journal of Education, No. 18.

‡ The Rationale of Political Representation, p. 216.

§ "Every one who has anything to lose which is worth the keeping, is a gainer by the education of the poorer classes. The safety of your Lordship's property, the well-being of society, the public security, depend upon the christian education of those classes."—Bp. of London's Speech on the Irish Church Bill, Aug. 24, 1835, p. 8.

We may add to this Mr. Simpson's axiom, "*There is but one time for moral training, and that is infancy.*"—p. 133.

When Milton took it in hand to write "of the reforming of education," he treats it as "one of the greatest and noblest designs that can be thought on, and for the want whereof this nation perishes." And he aimed at nothing less than "to point out the right path of a *virtuous and noble education*, laborious indeed at the first ascent, but else so smooth, so green, so full of goodly prospect and melodious sounds on every side, that the harp of Orpheus was not more charming."* Since the time of our divine poet, we may hope that a partial advance has been made to the attainment of this "goodly prospect;" but as respects the great bulk of the youthful population, we have yet to discover and agree upon the best mode of imparting to them a virtuous and noble education;†—an education which shall give the children of every class an accurate knowledge of their true position in society, and shall impress them with the conviction, that "all their faculties and blessings, their senses, talents, and reason, are held either for use or abuse; either to be ill or well employed: and that they will accordingly reap the fruits, either of their diligence or of their neglect."

This is not the place to discuss the question of the expediency of compulsory education by the state;—"a question which seems dependent on the general circumstances of a country, and which must be determined by social and political diversities rather than by universal and inflexible principles." But without calling for its interference to such an extent as this, we may consistently urge the duty of the state to promote the cause of education in other ways, particularly by grants in aid of voluntary donations, and by the establishment of Normal schools for the education of *well-qualified teachers*. At present we have masters to teach what they know but indifferently themselves, and one of the highest offices a human being can perform is frequently entrusted to persons who can bring no certificate of their proficiency, and whose low qualifications effectually degrade what should be a high and honourable profession.‡ "It is the

* Letter to Mr. Samuel Hartlib, 1650.

† Less perhaps to *discover* than to *realize*. The complete and luminous developement of the *principles* of a sound education suited to all classes,—in its threefold division of physical, intellectual, and moral,—for which we are indebted to Mr. Simpson, must leave us as a people without excuse in continuing longer in the old ways, which in this instance at least, experience proves to be those of error and disappointment. No one can rise from the perusal of Mr. S.'s work without the conviction that he has laid open the true path to national improvement, and that if we neglect longer the manly culture of the popular mind, "the sin lieth at our door." Were not Mr. S. "one who is above the pursuit of praise," the cordial admiration of his labours which his countrymen have publicly expressed, would be all that he could desire: but his enlightened patriotism will find its best reward in the testimony of conscience and in the anticipation of those blessings, which his country will ultimately derive from his exertions.

‡ "Until some care be taken to give the same security by law for the health of the mind, as is given for the health of the body; until schoolmasters are subjected

cautious and systematic selection of persons adapted for the office of teachers (says Mrs. Trollope, alluding to the Prussian system,) which can alone ensure a profitable national education."* "No system (says Professor Pillans) would work well without a good master, and it is upon this account that I conceive the institution of *schools for masters* to be at the foundation of all improvement in national education."† Another important step (as many writers have suggested)‡ would be the appointment of a *public functionary*, invested with similiar powers to those of the French Minister of Instruction, or of the Superintendant of common schools in the state of New York, who might give his undivided attention to those duties at present very partially and imperfectly discharged by the Home Department. Such an officer would find ample employment for a time in the collection of the *Statistics of education*; and besides his attention to the establishment of schools, he should have to watch over the working of them, to "improve their system of superintendence and plans of instruction, and to extend their sphere of action to the very limit of their means." An early result of the establishment of such an office, it is said, "would be to make the fact as well-known to ourselves as it already is to our neighbours, that in few countries of Europe are the elements of a *sound and useful instruction* so scantily diffused as in England and the sister island."§ The Select Committee on secondary punishments (of 1831) in noticing the general conduct of criminals in London, state that "most of them can read and write, but they are excessively *ignorant*; their reading and writing gives them no sort of knowledge; it is the same as if they could not read or write *as to any useful knowledge*."||

to at least as rigid a scrutiny as apothecaries, it is perfect nonsense to talk of education having failed to check the progress of crime in England,"...."a country, by the way, in which the science of education is at a lower ebb than in any other civilized nation on the earth."—For. Quar. Rev. Oct. 1835.

* Belgium ii. 169.

† "A crazy and ragged orator some time ago applied at the Mansion House for a few shillings and a pair of shoes, to take him *back* to Ireland, seeing he had found the pretensions of this island to learning exceedingly hollow. In his harangue to the Lord Mayor, he observed with exquisite and most appropriate sarcasm, 'that he had heard much of the schoolmaster being abroad in England, but that he had not had the good fortune to find any body *who had met with him!*'"—Simpson, p. 185.

‡ Quar. Jour. Ed.—Edinb. Rev. No. 117.—Simpson on Education, 214, &c.

§ Quar. Jour. Ed. No. 18, p. 327.

|| Guerry, p. 49.

"It forms an instructive example of the sedative effect of established habits of thinking, that our ancestors and ourselves have so contentedly held THIS to be education, or the shadow of it, for any rank of society! Reading, writing, and ciphering, are mere instruments: when attained, as they rarely or never are after all, by the working class to a reasonable perfection, they leave the pupil exactly in the situation where he would find himself, were we to put tools into his hands, the

With what success a national system of a far superior character to any with which we are familiar can be established and worked, is shown in the admirable report of Victor Cousin on the Prussian system of education,—a system beyond doubt, though not perfect,* the most vigorous and complete that has hitherto been put in operation on an extensive scale.† We are bound therefore to anticipate that in due time its results will be proportionately beneficial, and that an improved state of public morals will be shown even by the criminal records of that country.

But, in judging of the value of education by the *state of crime* in any community, it must be recollected that we are supplying at best but a *negative* test. It is almost impossible to appreciate the influence of the other causes simultaneously operating on public morals, and which may either neutralize the good effects of education, or positively outweigh them on the opposite side. Thus education may appear in some instances to have exercised little influence on the state of crime, where nevertheless, could we abstract that influence, other circumstances being unchanged, the moral condition of the people would have been even *worse* than we find it. We have seen that in the *northern* region of France, where instruction is far more prevalent than in the *centre*, the crimes against *property* relatively to the population are at least twice as numerous; but it is in the northern region also, although most abounding in *wealth* (and of course in temptations and opportunities for theft) that *pauperism* is most prevalent; and it is fair to conclude, that indigence and misery are the chief causes of its disproportionate share of crimes, which, under such circumstances, might be even *more* numerous were not instruction so generally diffused as it is. On the other hand, criminal statistics afford us no direct means of judging of the influence of education in civilizing and refining the manners, in creating new sources of occupation and enjoyment, and in repressing many vicious habits which materially interfere with the happiness and welfare of a community, though they may not be considered in our estimate of *crime*. The influence of instruction in this way is quiet and unnoticed, but we cannot doubt that it is powerful and extensive. This is true of even the first elements of education, as he that can read is at once made

use of which however he must learn as he may.... If a national system of education is to stop here, it would save much trouble and after disappointment not to attempt it at all."—Simpson, pp. 34, 35.

* See Mr. Simpson's strictures on the too exclusive importance allotted to the machinery, &c. pp. 215, 224.

† France is proceeding rapidly in the establishment of a similar system, with such modifications as to the enlightened superintendence of M. Guizot seem desirable. The grant of 1833 for national education was £600,000. The British legislature in the same year voted £20,000 for the same purpose,—a sum, as Mr. Simpson well remarks, only valuable as "an evidence of the *animus* of the government, and as a test of the feelings of the public."—p. 263.

more independent of extrinsic sources of enjoyment, and may learn to find in

> "*books*—a real world
> Round which, with tendrils strong as flesh and blood,
> His pastime and his happiness may grow."

"It is for want of innocent recreation," says a periodical writer already quoted,* "that the gin shop and ale-house are frequented: *unemployed* man requires *some* stimulant: he cannot work all his time, and if for want of instruction, he has not the power of enjoying pleasures of an innocent description, tippling, as it needs no talents or training, is invariably resorted to. It excites and stimulates; and what if health is impaired? The passing of his time in the enjoyment of even this low pleasure is to him preferable to that *weariness of mind* which proceeds from vacancy."

We must not enlarge further on this topic, which trite as it is, can never be considered by any one alive to the interests of humanity, as of slight importance or devoid of interest. We acknowledge (with Sir James Mackintosh) "that of all the fine arts, the noblest is the art of forming a vigorous, healthy, and beautiful mind;"† and although we have not the satisfaction of yet witnessing all the good effects which we believe education will ultimately produce, we cannot lose our faith in its efficacy to improve mankind. We scruple not therefore to conclude in the language of an eloquent writer‡:—

"That *knowledge* is an appreciable good for every being who is capable of knowledge: a good for the richest—a good for the poorest—a good for all who are placed in any part of the scale between the extremes of wealth and poverty:—that the only danger is, lest it should not be communicated with the requisite universality to the whole mass of the population, and in a sufficient amount to every individual member:—that *ignorance* on the

* Quarterly Journal of Education, No. 18, p. 237.

† Memoirs, i. 428.

‡ British Critic, Jan. 1835, p. 66.

At the risk of transgressing my prescribed bounds, I am tempted to add the following beautiful passage from Hartley Coleridge, as it is pregnant with political and moral wisdom: "Considering man as a person, consider him as *sentient*, *intelligent*, *moral*, and *immortal*. For simply to think of a man as a *sentient* being is inconsistent with that hard-hearted policy which would employ him, reckless of his suffering or enjoyment, like a wedge or a rivet, to build up the idol temple of a false national greatness; to regard him as *intelligent*, or rather as *capable of intelligence*, condemns the system that would keep him in ignorance to serve the purposes of his rulers, as game-cocks are penned up in the dark, that they may fight the better; to regard him as *moral*, corrects the primary conception of national prosperity; and to revere him as *immortal* commands preremptorily that he shall never be made a tool or an instrument to any end in which his own permanent welfare is not included."—Worthies of Yorkshire, p. 7.

contrary is the great degrader, and brutalizer, and corrupter of man; and that you will do more for the happiness of a human being, and put ampler means and implements and resources of enjoyment within his reach, by simply teaching him to read and write, and giving him a taste for mental pleasures, than by flinging millions of money into his lap and shutting him out at the same time from the pale of intellectual cultivation."

Printed in the USA
CPSIA information can be obtained
at www.ICGtesting.com
LVHW080425071123
763186LV00005B/409

9 781340 514006